Compare & Contrast

Teaching Comparative Thinking to
Strengthen Student Learning

MANUFACTURED WITH
100% WIND ENERGY

Compare & Contrast

Teaching Comparative Thinking to Strengthen Student Learning

Harvey F. Silver

Alexandria, Virginia USA

A GUIDE FOR PROFESSIONAL LEARNING COMMUNITIES

1703 N. Beauregard St. • Alexandria, VA 22311-1714 USA
Phone: 800-933-2723 or 703-578-9600 • Fax: 703-575-5400
Web site: www.ascd.org • E-mail: member@ascd.org
Author guidelines: www.ascd.org/write

Gene R. Carter, *Executive Director;* Nancy Modrak, *Publisher;* Scott Willis, *Director, Book Acquisitions & Development;* Julie Houtz, *Director, Book Editing & Production;* Miriam Goldstein, *Editor;* Georgia Park, *Senior Graphic Designer;* Mike Kalyan, *Production Manager;* Cynthia Stock, *Typesetter;* Kyle Steichen, *Production Specialist*

Printed in the United States of America. Cover art © 2010 by ASCD. ASCD publications present a variety of viewpoints. The views expressed or implied in this book should not be interpreted as official positions of the Association.

All Web links in this book are correct as of the publication date below but may have become inactive or otherwise modified since that time. If you notice a deactivated or changed link, please e-mail books@ascd.org with the words "Link Update" in the subject line. In your message, please specify the Web link, the book title, and the page number on which the link appears.

PAPERBACK ISBN: 978-1-4166-1058-8   ASCD product #110126   n6/10

Quantity discounts for the paperback edition only: 10–49 copies, 10%; 50+ copies, 15%; for 1,000 or more copies, call 800-933-2723, ext. 5634, or 703-575-5634. For desk copies: member@ascd.org.

Library of Congress Cataloging-in-Publication Data

Silver, Harvey F.
    Compare & contrast : teaching comparative thinking to strengthen student learning / Harvey F. Silver.
        p. cm. — (A strategic teacher PLC guide)
    Includes bibliographical references and index.
    ISBN 978-1-4166-1058-8 (pbk. : alk. paper)
    1. Blended learning—Cross-cultural studies. 2. Educational technology—Cross-cultural studies. 3. Comparative education. I. Title.
    LB1028.5.S4955 2010
    371.39—dc22
                                                                        2010010563

20 19 18 17 16 15 14 13 12 11 10   1 2 3 4 5 6 7 8 9 10 11 12

It is difficult to imagine this work having taken shape without the wisdom of our dear and deeply missed friend, Richard Strong. Richard's brilliant work in helping schools become better and more thoughtful places will continue to inspire us.

Compare & Contrast

Teaching Comparative Thinking to Strengthen Student Learning

Acknowledgments

Action Research Team

Joyce Wagers Jackson
Susan C. Morris
Daniel R. Moirao, Ed.D
Victor Klein
Barb Heinzman

The work of these Thoughtful Classroom trainers and coaches in schools across the country played a critical role in the development of the Strategic Teacher PLC Guides. The feedback the team brought back from teachers, teacher leaders, and administrators made each successive version—and there were many versions—more powerful and more practical for educators.

Special thanks go to the Green River Regional Educational Cooperative (GRREC) in Kentucky, where earlier versions of these Strategic Teacher PLC Guides were piloted with more than 100 schools. It was the vision of teacher leadership shared by Liz Storey, Jamie Spugnardi, and hundreds of other teacher leaders and administrators from GRREC schools that helped us realize the potential of this new approach to building professional learning communities in schools.

To the wonderful staff at ASCD—Nancy Modrak, Ann Cunningham-Morris, Julie Houtz, Jean Pride, Deborah Brown, Genny Ostertag, Miriam Goldstein, and many others—thank you for your support and enthusiasm for these new products we call Strategic Teacher PLC Guides. But the greatest debt of thanks goes to Scott Willis. Without Scott's guidance and his ability to see the big picture and think through the details, we don't know where we'd be.

Finally, for never letting us—or our schools—forget the central role that thought plays in every act of teaching and learning, we would like to thank Art Costa and Bena Kallick. We are proud to integrate your work in building students' habits of mind into these Strategic Teacher PLC Guides.

Introduction

A New Professional Development Tool

You're holding a new kind of professional development tool called a Strategic Teacher PLC Guide. Designed in partnership with more than 75 schools, Strategic Teacher PLC Guides make the important work of bringing high-impact, research-based instructional practices into every classroom easier than ever before. Each guide focuses on one research-based strategy and serves as a complete professional development resource for a team of teachers to learn, plan, and implement the strategy in their classrooms.

This Strategic Teacher PLC Guide focuses on Compare & Contrast, a critical thinking strategy unique in its capacity to build students' memories, eliminate confusion, and highlight crucial similarities and differences. As educational researchers Robert Marzano, Debra Pickering, and Jane Pollock (2001) report in *Classroom Instruction That Works*, comparative thinking strategies are the single most effective way to improve student learning, leading to an *average percentile gain of 45 points* in student achievement. Compare & Contrast takes the natural human capacity to make comparisons and maximizes its effectiveness by leading students through a four-phase learning process that involves

- Describing each item separately using criteria.

- Capturing key similarities and differences on a comparison organizer.

- Forming and discussing generalizations and conclusions.

- Synthesizing learning by completing a relevant task.

The Compare & Contrast strategy also integrates the habits of mind—a set of dispositions that increase students' capacity for skillful thinking (Costa & Kallick, 2008, 2009).

Turning Knowledge into Practice

Here are three things we know about improving teaching and learning:

1. High-quality instruction leads invariably to higher levels of student achievement. Most educational researchers have concluded that the quality of classroom instruction is the single greatest determinant of student success.

2. High-quality instruction is replicable. There are specific, research-based strategies that are proven to raise student achievement—and that all teachers can master with time and support.

3. Schools that function as effective professional learning communities see "big, often immediate, dividends in student learning and professional morale in virtually any setting" (Schmoker, 2005, p. xii).

In other words, we know that we need to focus on improving instruction, we know which strategies will work, and we know that professional learning communities are key to any such efforts. But knowing these statements to be true doesn't mean that change is easy. In fact, we have worked with thousands of teachers and administrators who have built professional development around research-based strategies and professional learning communities, only to be disappointed by the results. Why? They were focused on the right things. They understood the crucial importance of collegial learning. What they needed was the *how*. *How do we make our professional learning communities work?*

The solution we developed with these schools is *learning clubs*. If you've been struggling to make the professional learning community concept a reality in your school, or if you're just beginning the process of establishing a professional learning community, learning clubs can help. A learning club is a collaborative support structure that makes the process of establishing and sustaining a professional learning community more manageable for teachers, administrators, and schools. A typical learning club consists of four to eight teachers who meet regularly to talk about and refine their instructional practices.

Learning Clubs and Strategic Teacher PLC Guides: Perfect Together

Over the years, we have found that the members of the most successful learning clubs follow a relatively standard set of guidelines to maximize the power of collaborative learning. In response, we designed the Strategic Teacher PLC Guides around these guidelines. The members of successful learning clubs

• *Concentrate on instructional techniques proven to make a difference*. That's why each Strategic Teacher PLC Guide focuses on a specific strategy backed by both research and classroom practice.

• *Learn new strategies interdependently*. That's why each Strategic Teacher PLC Guide has been designed for use by a team of teachers. Discussion, group reflection, and group processing activities are all built into its structure.

• *Use new strategies in their classrooms*. That's why each Strategic Teacher PLC Guide puts such a high premium on classroom application. Teachers plan lessons, implement them in the classroom, and evaluate the results together.

• *Bring student work back to their learning clubs*. That's why each Strategic Teacher PLC Guide includes one full section dedicated to the analysis of student work.

• *Self-assess throughout the process.* That's why each Strategic Teacher PLC Guide includes strategy implementation milestones that teachers can use to determine where they are and where they need to go next.

But Where Will We Find the Time?

As the research of Bruce Joyce and Beverly Showers (2002) makes clear, learning a new strategy is never as simple as attending a workshop or reading a chapter in a book. If you expect to implement a new strategy successfully in the classroom, then you'll need to commit at least 10–12 hours of embedded professional development time to master that strategy. Here's how some of the schools we work with address the challenge of time:

• Some schools convert their staff meetings, grade-level meetings, or department meetings into learning club sessions.

• Some schools use a portion of their committed professional development days for learning clubs.

• Some schools create intensive summer sessions for their learning clubs.

• Some schools have made a full commitment to the power of job-embedded learning and set aside regular time for learning clubs to meet on a weekly, biweekly, or monthly basis.

Because each school has unique scheduling demands and professional development resources, Strategic Teacher PLC Guides provide maximum flexibility. This guide, for example, is divided into four separate sections:

• Section 1 serves as an introductory tutorial on Compare & Contrast. Between Sections 1 and 2, teachers look for opportunities to incorporate comparative thinking into their instruction.

• Section 2 shows teachers how to plan and implement a Compare & Contrast lesson in their classrooms. Between Sections 2 and 3, teachers implement their lessons in the classroom and work with a critical friend to provide reciprocal feedback on their lessons.

• In Section 3, teachers reflect on how their lessons worked in the classroom. Between Sections 3 and 4, teachers design and implement a new lesson and collect samples of student work.

• Section 4 models a process for analyzing student work and shows teachers how to use this student work to improve instructional decision making.

We recommend that you preview these four sections and develop a schedule that works for all the members in your learning club. *As a final note, make sure you photocopy the lesson planning forms before filling them out (see pp. 42–44). You will need more blank forms as you plan future lessons.*

Good luck and good learning!

Why Compare & Contrast?

This section serves as an introductory tutorial on the Compare & Contrast strategy. In this section, our goal is to help you understand how you currently use comparative thinking in your classroom and to explain the Strategic Teacher approach to the Compare & Contrast strategy.

In this section you will

- Reflect on your own experiences with comparative thinking strategies.

- Explore the research, principles, and classroom phases that make Compare & Contrast such an effective strategy.

- Examine a range of student work that demonstrates comparative thinking.

- Experience a model lesson using the Compare & Contrast strategy.

Let's Get Started

Comparative thinking is one of our first and most natural forms of thought. When we are infants, one of the first differences we must identify is that between mother and other. Without the ability to make comparisons—to set one object or idea against another and take note of similarities and differences—much of what we call learning would quite literally be impossible.

You may be wondering why we want to look so closely at comparative thinking. What makes it so special? The answer lies in the research of renowned educators Robert Marzano, Debra Pickering, and Jane Pollock (2001). By compiling the available research on effective instruction, Marzano, Pickering, and Pollock found that strategies that engage students in comparative thinking had the greatest effect on student achievement, leading to an *average percentile gain of 45 points* (p. 7f). More recently, Marzano's research in *The Art and Science of Teaching* (2007) reconfirmed that asking students to identify similarities and differences through comparative analysis leads to eye-opening gains in student achievement.

Although comparative thinking is a natural operation of our minds and is essential to learning, most students have a difficult time making use of comparisons in school. To better understand how to achieve success when asking your students to make comparisons, it is important to first understand your own attitude toward comparisons and how you use them in your classroom. Keeping that in mind, take a moment to answer the questions below:

Activity: How Do You Use Comparisons?

1. Why Compare & Contrast? What use does it have in your classroom?

2. In what situations do you feel comparison works well?

3. What are the steps you use in teaching students how to make comparisons?

4. What might your students' work be like if they made better comparisons?

What Can Compare & Contrast Do for You and Your Students?

Compare & Contrast helps teachers achieve five distinct instructional goals:

GOAL #1:   **Strengthen Students' Memories**
By focusing student thinking on analyzing pairs of ideas, the Compare & Contrast strategy strengthens students' ability to remember key content.

GOAL #2:   **Develop Higher-Order Thinking Skills**
Compare & Contrast acts as a practical and easy-to-use introduction to higher-order thinking.

GOAL #3:   **Increase Student Comprehension**
Compare & Contrast improves comprehension by highlighting important details, making abstract ideas more concrete, and reducing the confusion between related concepts (think *meiosis* versus *mitosis*).

GOAL #4:   **Enhance Students' Writing in the Content Areas**
The Compare & Contrast strategy strengthens students' writing skills by providing a simple structure that helps them organize information and develop their ideas with greater clarity and precision.

GOAL #5:   **Develop Students' Habits of Mind**
In their years of research into the defining characteristics of intelligent behavior and thought, Art Costa and Bena Kallick (2008, 2009) have identified 16 "habits of mind." By nourishing these habits in our students, we give them the tools they need to use their minds well, thus increasing their chance for future success. Using Compare & Contrast in the classroom will help students develop these habits of mind: thinking flexibly; thinking about thinking (metacognition); striving for accuracy; applying past knowledge to new situations; and thinking and communicating with clarity and precision.

Answer the question below and then discuss your answer with your neighbor.

Activity: The Most Important Goal

Which of the five goals of the Compare & Contrast strategy is most important to you, and why?

A Potpourri of Classroom Comparisons

The next few pages show the kinds of work students create while engaged in Compare & Contrast lessons. Figure 1.1 includes a variety of student work samples that span a wide range of content areas and grade levels. As you examine this work, ask yourself, What skills are students demonstrating in this work?

Figure 1.1   **Compare & Contrast Potpourri**

A 3rd grader analyzes the structure of two fables.

"The Tortoise and the Hare"	Criteria	"The Tortoise and the Antelope"
A tortoise A hare	Characters	A tortoise Antelope
Because the hare makes fun of the tortoise	Why they decide to race	Because they argue who can go faster
The hare goes to sleep by accident	How the tortoise wins	The tortoise and some friends trick the antelope
"slow and steady wins the race"	Lesson	"Team work works"

A 1st grader uses a magnifying glass to identify the critical attributes of coins.

Name of Coin	penny	nickel	dime	quarter
Color	copper	silver	silver	silver
Shape	circle	circle	circle	circle
Size	medium	large	small	largest
How Edges Feel	smooth	smooth	bumpy	bumpy
Year	1991	1975	1967	1990
President on Front	Lincoln	Jefferson	Truman	Washington
Picture on Back of Regular Coin	building	building	torch plants	eagle
Picture on Back of NJ Coin	X	X	X	crossing Delaware
Value	1¢	5¢	10¢	25¢

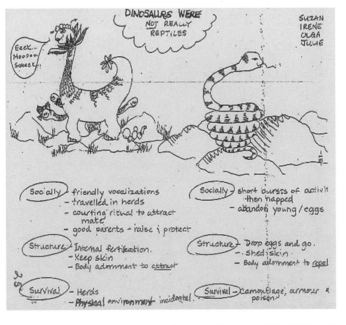

A group of middle school students use words and images to distinguish reptiles from dinosaurs.

Figure 1.1 (*continued*)

A high school student creates a T-Shirt Organizer to identify the similarities and differences between anaerobic and aerobic exercise.

A middle school student creates a Top Hat Organizer to summarize and review critical similarities and differences between volume and surface area.

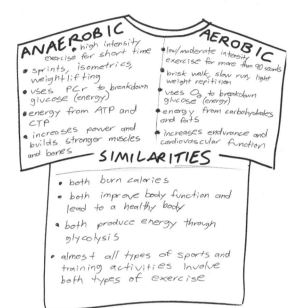

ANAEROBIC
- high intensity exercise for short time
- sprints, isometrics, weightlifting
- uses PCr to breakdown glucose (energy)
- energy from ATP and CTP
- increases power and builds stronger muscles and bones

AEROBIC
- low/moderate intensity exercise for more than 90 seconds
- brisk walk, slow run, light weight repetition
- uses O₂ to breakdown glucose (energy)
- energy from carbohydrates and fats
- increases endurance and cardiovascular function

SIMILARITIES
- both burn calories
- both improve body function and lead to a healthy body
- both produce energy through glycolysis
- almost all types of sports and training activities involve both types of exercise

Volume

Volume is the measurement of space a three-dimensional figure occupies.

Always involves multiplying area of the base by height of the figure.

Expressed in cubic units

Often used to figure out how much containers can hold (e.g., water in a swimming pool)

Surface Area

Surface area is the sum of all the surfaces of a three-dimensional figure.

Always involves adding up the areas of the individual surfaces.

Expressed in square units

Often used to figure out how much covering is needed (e.g., paint or wrapping paper)

Similarities
Both apply to three-dimensional shapes.
Both require you to know how to find two-dimensional area

A high school student compares the educational philosophies of Booker T. Washington and W. E. B. Du Bois on a Y Organizer.

Booker T. Washington
- believed in education in agriculture and industry
- wanted to help blacks become self-reliant and competent tradespeople
- willing to accomodate current views on race; didn't want to "rock the boat"
- created the Tuskegee Institute in 1881 to train African Americans in trades and agriculture

W. E. B. Du Bois
- believed in education in the liberal arts and higher education
- wanted to develop more black leaders and intellectuals
- advocating directly confronting issues of segregation and racism
- helped found the NAACP in 1909

Similarities
- both were great leaders
- both were concerned about limited opportunities for blacks
- both believed education was the best way to achieve equality

Figure 1.1 (*continued*)

A 5th grader draws conclusions about renewable and nonrenewable energy.

The most important difference between renewable energy and nonrenewable energy is that renewable energy won't run out, while nonrenewable energy will eventually run out

Possible cause(s) for this difference is/are renewable energy comes from sources like wind, the sun, and plants that come back and that can't run out. Nonrenewable energy comes from sources like coal and fossil fuels that don't come back after they're taken

Possible effect(s) of this difference is/are The U.S. and other countries are trying to find new ways to develop renewable energy sources because people will need renewable energy in the future when nonrenewable sources run out.

A 2nd grader creates a Flip Strip to show how frogs and toads differ.

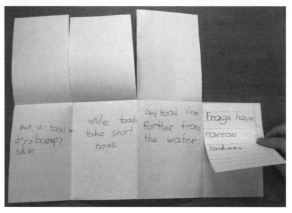

A 2nd grader writes a simple comparison essay on spheres and rectangular prisms.

Let's find out about how the sphere and the rectanglar prism are different and alike! First of all the word vertices means corners. A sphere and a rectanglar prism are alike because they are 3-D shapes. The way that they are different are that ~~the prism~~ the sphere can roll while the prism doesn't. The prism has vertices and the sphere doesn't. The sphere doesn't have edges and the prism does. The prism has faces and the sphere doesn't. Also the prism has flat basses while the sphere doesn't. How do you think they are alike and different?

What skills were evident in these student work samples? Use the space below to record your thoughts, then discuss your response with a partner.

Activity: Looking at the Skills

Skills:

We all want our students to produce this kind of work—to be able to use comparative thinking independently to advance their own learning. To help us achieve this goal, let's turn our attention to the four principles and the four phases of Compare & Contrast. Each principle is tied closely to the difficulties students commonly encounter when they engage in comparative thinking. You'll notice that the four *principles* of Compare & Contrast are closely aligned with the four classroom *phases* of Compare & Contrast. Leading your students through these four phases is essential for ensuring your students' effective use of the Compare & Contrast strategy in the classroom. A classroom poster highlighting these four phases for students is included in this guide. Figure 1.2 shows the four principles and corresponding four phases of Compare & Contrast.

Figure 1.2   **The Four Principles and Phases of Compare & Contrast**

Principle One: Know the Purpose and the Content

Many students flounder when asked to make comparisons because they . . .

- Don't know why they're making a comparison.

- Aren't given the chance to get to know the items or ideas before comparing.

- Don't know what to look for when describing the items or ideas.

Phase One: Description

- Begin with a hook that helps students activate and apply base knowledge to the learning at hand. For example, "Does anyone know what an underdog is? What are some examples of underdogs we can think of? Why do we root for underdogs?"

- Connect the discussion generated by the hook to the purpose of the lesson. For example, "Today we are going to read two fables about underdogs. As we read, we're going to use the Compare & Contrast strategy to figure out what's similar about the fables, how they're different, and what the differences might tell us about the lesson each fable is trying to teach us."

- Remind the students that their job is to describe the items separately, not to compare them yet. Model the description process.

- Provide clear criteria to focus student descriptions and a simple description organizer (see below). Encourage students to strive for accuracy as they use the criteria to collect information.

"The Tortoise and the Hare"	Criteria	"The Tortoise and the Antelope"
	Characters	
	Why They Decide to Race	
	How the Tortoise Wins	
	Lesson	

Figure 1.2 (*continued*)

Principle Two: Thoughts Need Time . . . and a Shape

Students live in a culture of speed, where one brief answer often gets the job done. But quality comparisons need time, nourishment, and a structure for teasing out the most important similarities and differences.

Phase Two: Comparison

- To increase students' capacity for thinking interdependently, consider allowing them to conduct comparisons in partnerships or small groups.

- Model good comparative thinking using everyday objects (e.g., a fork and a spoon).

- Remind students to use their descriptions and criteria from Phase One to guide their search for similarities and differences.

- Provide a visual organizer (see below) that allows students to line up parallel differences. For example, "The fast animal is a hare/The fast animal is an antelope."

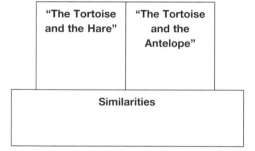

Principle Three: And the Verdict Is . . .

Too often, classroom comparisons stop abruptly, as though comparison is the end of the process. But students need to use their comparison—to draw their own conclusions and discuss those conclusions—if the comparison is to be meaningful.

Phase Three: Conclusion

Use questions that stretch students' minds and that compel them to draw conclusions about the items. For example, for the lesson on fables, you might pose this question: "Are the two fables more alike or more different?" Other kinds of concluding questions in other content areas might sound like this:

- What's the most important difference between renewable and nonrenewable energy? What are the possible causes for this difference? What are the possible effects?

- What can you conclude about three-dimensional shapes?

Allow students to discuss, defend, and refine their conclusions.

Figure 1.2 (*continued*)

Principle Four: Put Learning to Work	Phase Four: Application
Knowledge left in pieces is easier to lose than knowledge that is made whole. That's why Compare & Contrast ends with a synthesis task asking students to pull together what they have learned and to apply that learning to the creation of a product.	Ask students to create a product that integrates what they have learned from the comparison. For example, "Imagine you are writing a fable about a race between a slow animal and a fast animal in which the slow animal wins. Which animals would you choose? How would you make the slow animal win? What lesson would your fable teach?" To increase students' capacity for metacognitive reflection, make time for them to look back on the different kinds of thinking they engaged in during the lesson. Lead a discussion in which students talk about their successes and struggles with different forms of thinking (describe, compare, draw conclusions, apply learning).

Now that you have a better understanding of the four phases of the Compare & Contrast strategy, take a second look at the student work samples in Figure 1.1. Each of the four phases is represented by at least one piece of student work. Can you determine which work samples were developed during which classroom phase?

The Strategy in Action

Now let's experience a lesson using the Compare & Contrast strategy. Joanne Glass, a high school history teacher, wants her students to understand how circumstances of time and place influence perspective. With this lesson, Joanne is looking to shift her students' attention from *macrohistory* to *microhistory*. Most students are familiar with the major events, dates, and people that make up macrohistory, but students are often not aware of the knowledge that can be gained from studying the microhistory of social customs, personal writings, and everyday lives of common people. To this end, Joanne has designed a lesson using Compare & Contrast based on two primary documents, one from a 17th century Puritan family and one about a 19th century industrial family. Joanne has made sure that the activities and assessments in the lesson require students to practice the skills assessed by her state's standardized tests, including

- The ability to present clear analyses of issues, ideas, texts, and experiences;

- The ability to support positions with well-developed arguments;

- The ability to develop arguments with effective use of details and evidence; and

- The ability to explain the importance of analyzing narratives and documents from different times and places to understand historical events.

The Model Lesson: Different Times, Different Households

As you review this lesson, keep in mind the principles of Compare & Contrast, the role of the student, the role of the teacher, and the goals of the strategy. We also encourage you to *be* the student by completing the student activities throughout the lesson.

The Hook and Bridge of the Lesson

The "hook and bridge" is meant to hook students into the lesson by creating bridges between students' prior knowledge or personal experiences and the content of the lesson. It also focuses students' attention in preparation for the lesson ahead.

Joanne begins her lesson by saying, "Stop and think about some families that you know. Have you ever noticed how some households are different from your own? Take a moment and jot down some ways in which households are similar and different from one another."

Activity: Comparing Households

How are households similar and different?

The Content: Two Readings, Two Households

Joanne continues, "In this lesson, we are going to go back into the 17th and 19th centuries, where you will have the opportunity to visit two homes. The first passage you will read is taken from a 17th century father's diary, and the second passage comes from a 19th century song. As you visit these homes, pay close attention to the following criteria: the father's role, the daughter's role, the nature of the world, and the nature of the home."

Two Images of Fatherhood

A 17th Century Father Talks to His Daughter

Recognizing that I, like all men, will one day perish, I invited my daughter, little Katy, into my study. I told my child that I am to die shortly, and she must, when I am dead, remember everything I said unto her. I set before her the sinful and woeful condition of her nature, and I charged her to pray in secret places every day without ceasing that God for the sake of Jesus Christ would give her a new heart. I wished her to live happily under God and abide by the laws governing her existence here. I gave her to understand that when I am taken from her she must look to meet with more humbling afflictions than she does now [when] she has a careful and tender father to provide for her.

"Father Is Coming" (19th Century Song)

The clock is on the stroke of six;
The father's work is done;
Sweep up the hearth and mend the fire,
And put the kettle on.
The wild night wind is blowing cold,
'Tis dreary crossing o'er the wold.

He is crossing o'er the wold apace,
He is stronger than the storm;
He does not feel the cold, not he,
His heart it is so warm;
For father's heart is stout and true
As ever human bosom knew. . . .

Nay, do not close the shutters, child;
For along the lane
The little window looks, and he
Can see it shining plain;
I've heard him say he loves to mark
The cheerful firelight through the dark. . . .

Hark! hark! I hear his footsteps now,
He's through the garden gate;
Run, little Bess, and open the door,
And do not let him wait;
Shout, baby, shout! and clap thy hands,
For father on the threshold stands.

You'll notice that even at this early stage of the lesson, students are engaged in addressing state standards by analyzing primary documents from different time periods.

Phase One: Description

Now Joanne asks students to use the criteria provided in the description organizer (see Figure 1.3) to describe each household.

You'll notice that we have added a section to the right for you to record your own thoughts on the lesson. This is part of a process we call "Do, Look, Learn." Too often, we go through the motions of learning a new process or idea without reflecting on our own thinking. As you "do" the lesson, "look" in on your own thought process to see what you can "learn" from your own experiences.

Figure 1.3 **Activity: Description Organizer**

17th Century Family	Criteria	19th Century Family	Your Thoughts . . .
	Father's Role		
	Daughter's Role		
	Nature of the Home		
	Nature of the World		

Thinking About Phase One: Thorough descriptions framed by clear criteria lead to deeper and richer comparisons. The more students are encouraged to think about details and specifics in their description, the easier and more sophisticated their comparisons will be. Take a moment to look back at the readings with the criteria from Figure 1.3 in mind. How do the criteria affect your thinking?

Note that *criteria* are not perfectly synonymous with *critical attributes*. Most comparison strategies ask students to focus their attention on critical attributes, which are the defining characteristics of the items under investigation. Critical attributes are always a good starting point for helping students to focus their attention on the essential information, but sometimes we want students to go beyond simply describing the items by these attributes. For example, if students are describing *renewable energy* and *nonrenewable energy,* we may want students to consider not only the critical attributes (e.g., the sources of the types of energy, how each type is used) but also the factors that put renewable and nonrenewable energy into a larger context (e.g., arguments for and against each type of energy).

Phase Two: Comparison

Joanne now moves her students into the comparison phase by having them work with partners to identify similarities and differences between the two households and then to record those similarities and differences using the Top Hat Organizer (see Figure 1.4).

Figure 1.4 **Activity: Top Hat Organizer**

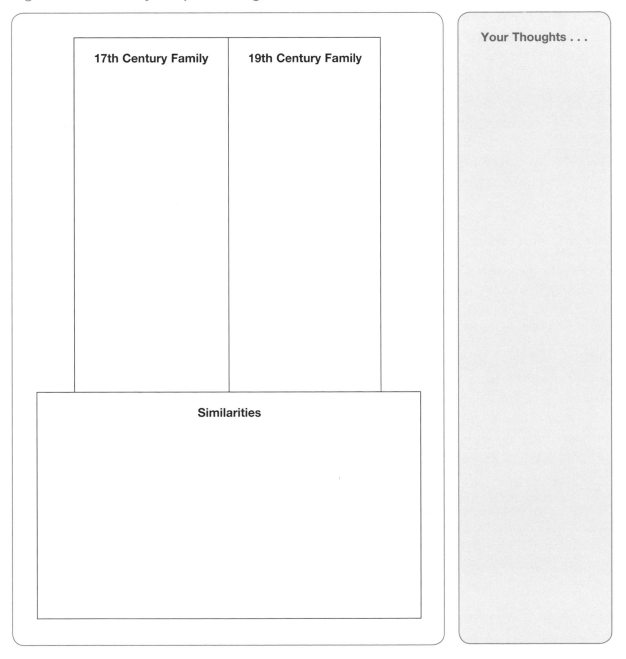

Thinking About Phase Two: Notice how much easier it was to conduct a comparison having already completed detailed descriptions of the readings. These first two phases encourage students to use details and evidence from the readings to support their comparisons, and the Top Hat Organizer helps students give their thoughts a shape.

Phase Three: Conclusion

For this phase, Joanne asks her students to discuss what they have learned as a result of their comparison and to form some conclusions. She uses the questions in Figure 1.5 to guide the discussion.

Figure 1.5   **Activity: Drawing Conclusions**

	Your Thoughts . . .
1. Are the two homes more alike or different? Explain your response.	
2. What do you suspect to be some of the causes for the differences between the homes?	
3. Based on the documents, what can you conclude to be the ideal traits of 17th century and 19th century fathers?	

Thinking About Phase Three: Guided by questions, students are forced to distill the evidence they have gathered from the passages and analyze the two readings in greater depth. By asking students to take a position and draw conclusions about the content, we enhance their retention and understanding.

Phase Four: Application

Joanne introduces her application activity by saying, "You have seen how specific time periods affect the notion of family and the roles of fathers and daughters. Now you will be asked to synthesize what you have learned in this lesson in a creative task. Think about today's society. How do our time period and culture affect the role that fathers play in our families?" Joanne then introduces and explains the following synthesis task.

Activity: Want Ad

> **Pick two universal traits for ideal fathers, whether they come from the 17th, the 19th, or the 21st century. Then pick two more traits that you believe are unique to modern fathers. Use the four traits you select to develop a want ad for an ideal 21st century father.**

Thinking About Phase Four: Remember the principle of "putting learning to work"? Creating a real-world task and asking students to stretch their thinking beyond the original context increases transfer and helps students find deeper meaning in the content.

Figure 1.6 depicts how one student group completed the four phases of the lesson. How does their work compare with yours?

Figure 1.6 **Student Work from the Lesson**

Description Phase

17th Century Family	Criteria	19th Century Family
moral guidance, teacher, spiritual leader, provider	**Father's Role**	worker, provider, care for family, be strong
to be obedient, affectionate, and pray every day	**Daughter's Role**	greet her father, take care of chores
strict, formal, religious, lawful	**Nature of the Home**	warm, friendly, safe, loving
filled with evil	**Nature of the World**	stormy, dreary, cold, dark

Comparison Phase

17th Century	19th Century
• Focused on God and religion	• Focused on providing for and protecting family
• Home was very strict and religious	• Home was very warm and inviting
• Father is watchful, always present	• Father must travel to work and provide for family
• Daughter is naturally sinful, needs to pray and obey her father	• Daughter has responsibilities around the home

Similarities

- Father is head of the household
- Home is a safe place
- The outside world is a threatening place
- The daughter is obedient to her father

Figure 1.6 (*continued*)

Conclusion Phase

1. **Are the two items more alike or different? Explain.** More different. The 19th century family seems to have a loving relationship. There is singing and excitement. The 17th century family is focused mostly on God and sin.

2. **What do you suspect to be some of the causes of the difference between the homes?** Seventeenth century America was more Puritanical. Life was focused on following the rules of religion. This made the home a strict place where fun was considered sinful. In the 19th century, the father works away from the home. After a hard day of work, the family looks forward to spending time together.

3. **Based on these documents, what can you conclude about the ideal traits of 17th century and 19th century fathers?**

   - 17th century: Disciplined, religious, keeps family focused on prayer, shows love by being honest, provider.

   - 19th century: Hard worker and provider, enjoys being with family, strong, caring, loving, determined.

Application Phase

Wanted:
A 21st Century Father Who Can Wear Many Hats, Including:

The "Loving Hat"

Responsibilities include: Raising children, not yelling, taking Mom out to romantic dinners, listening, "being there."

Benefits: You'll be loved right back.

The "Money Hat"

Responsibilities include: Holding down a good job, making enough money to support family and pay for vacations.

Benefits: Who doesn't want a good job? Plus, vacations with the family.

The "Fun Hat"

Responsibilities include: Taking family to baseball games in summer, going sleigh riding in winter, being goofy, dancing.

Benefits: What good is life if you don't have any fun? Family outings become memories that last a lifetime.

The "Handyman Hat"

Responsibilities include: Taking care of the house and yard. Must know basic carpentry, landscaping, plumbing, and electrical work.

Benefits: You'll get to have a really cool set of tools, including power tools.

THOUGHTWORK

Before the Next Section

Take a moment to reflect on what you covered in this section by answering the questions below.

Activity: Reflecting on Section 1

1. How did the strategy help Joanne to achieve her goals?

2. How did the phases of the strategy support the principles of the strategy?

3. How is the Compare & Contrast strategy similar to what you already do with your students when you want them to engage in comparison? How is it different?

In the next section, you will be planning your own Compare & Contrast lesson. To prepare, you should do the following things before you move on:

• Keep an eye out for students who use comparative thinking in your classroom. What steps do you notice them taking? How comfortable are they with comparison?

• As you teach over the coming weeks, keep track of those times when you might have used Compare & Contrast. Take note of these instances, and be ready to share them as you proceed through the following sections.

• Compile all the materials you'll need to plan a Compare & Contrast lesson (e.g., content, standards to cover) and bring them to the next meeting with your learning club.

Planning a Lesson

The goal in this section is to work with a partner to develop a lesson for your students.

In this section you will

- Learn from sample lessons designed by other teachers.

- Plan a complete lesson using the Compare & Contrast strategy and the content you have brought with you.

- Learn classroom tips for the effective implementation of Compare & Contrast in your classroom.

Here's a quick way to get into the comparative groove for this section. Figure 2.1 is a list of more than 100 paired topics, organized by content area, that make for rich Compare & Contrast lessons. Review the list, focusing on your content area. Which topics for lessons intrigue you the most? At the bottom of the figure, you'll see a space labeled "Other Lesson Ideas" for your own ideas. Can you generate at least three more topics from your content area that would make for fruitful Compare & Contrast lessons?

Figure 2.1 **Compare & Contrast Topics**

English/Language Arts

Noun–Verb

Prefix–Suffix

Myth–Fairy Tale

Sentence–Paragraph

Comedy–Drama

Novel–Short Story

Present Tense–Past Tense

Dependent Clause–Independent Clause

Semicolon–Colon

Blank Verse–Free Verse

R. Frost's "Design"–L. Hughes's "Harlem"

Hamlet–Holden Caulfield

Emerson–Thoreau

Naturalism–Realism

Winnie the Pooh–Piglet

Macbeth–Othello

Irregular Verb–Regular Verb

Science

Frog–Toad

Life Cycle–Seasons

Summer–Winter

Heart–Lungs

Metal–Wood

Compass–Clock

Star–Planet

Phenotype–Genotype

Earth–Mars

Galileo–Edison

Volcano–Earthquake

Renewable Energy–Nonrenewable Energy

Amphibian–Reptile

Vertebrate–Invertebrate

Deciduous–Conifer

Bacteria–Virus

Comet–Asteroid

Jurassic–Mesozoic

Plant Cell–Animal Cell

Mitosis–Meiosis

Fission–Fusion

Chemical Change–Physical Change

Acid–Base

Newton–Einstein

Gamma Radiation–Radio Waves

Kinetic Energy–Potential Energy

Social Studies/Geography

Atlantic–Pacific

Mississippi–Nile

Sparta–Athens

Great Wall of China–Pyramids at Giza

Latitude–Longitude

Desert–Jungle

Rockies–Andes

Byzantine–Roman

Napoleon–Alexander the Great

Marco Polo–Columbus

Jefferson–Adams

Constitution–Articles of Confederation

Revolutionary War–Civil War

Imperialism–Isolationism

Capitalism–Communism

Constitution–Magna Carta

World War I–World War II

Malcolm X–Martin Luther King Jr.

American Revolution–French Revolution

Western Feudalism–Japanese Feudalism

Knight–Samurai

Whigs–Tories

Teddy Roosevelt–Franklin D. Roosevelt

Spice Road–Northwest Passage

Algonquin–Iroquois

Maya–Aztec

Colosseum–Parthenon

House–Senate

Figure 2.1 (*continued*)

Mathematics
Addition–Subtraction
Multiplication–Division
Even Numbers–Odd Numbers
Analog Clock–Digital Watch
Arabic Numerals–Roman Numerals
Circle–Square
Cone–Cube
Fractions–Decimals
Trapezoid–Parallelogram
Numerator–Denominator
Decimal–Whole Number
Area–Perimeter
Simple Integer–Complex Integer
Volume–Area
Rational Number–Irrational Number
Solving for *t*–Solving for *d*
Linear Equation–Quadratic Equation
Sine–Cosine
Logs–Exponents
Leibniz–Newton
Bell Curve–Dumbbell

Fine Arts
Clarinet–Trumpet
Sculpture–Painting
Major–Minor Scale
Orchestra–Ensemble
Impressionism–Cubism
Van Gogh–Picasso
Baroque–Neoclassical
Beethoven–Mozart
Beatles–Elvis Presley

Sonata–Symphony
Digital Photography–Film Photography
Video Editing–Copyediting

Career & Technical Education
Marketing–Advertising
Disc Brakes–Drum Brakes
Poaching–Boiling
Julienne–Chiffonade
Closed Circuit–Open Circuit
Low-Voltage Wiring–High-Voltage Wiring
Registered Nurse–Nurse Practitioner
"Hard" Skills–"Soft" Skills
MRI–X-Ray
Gasoline Engine–Diesel Engine

Miscellaneous
Survey–Poll
Jung–Freud
Norms–Mores
Isometrics–Weight Training
Recession–Depression
Money Market–CD
Keynes–Smith
Bridge–Tunnel
Architect–Engineer
Editorial–Article
Mac–PC
Linux–Windows
HTML–Java Script
Tennis–Badminton
Ser–Estar
Day of the Dead–Halloween

Other Lesson Ideas

Learning from Sample Lessons

This activity serves as an introduction to planning a lesson using the Compare & Contrast strategy.

On the following pages, you will find four sample Compare & Contrast lessons on the topics of *tall tales* (English/language arts), *simple and compound interest* (mathematics), *aerobic and anaerobic exercise* (physical education/science), and *the poetry of the Civil Rights Movement* (English/U.S. history). For each lesson, we have provided both a description of what the lesson looks like in the classroom and the teacher's lesson plan, which provides insight into the thinking that went into the lesson. To increase each learning club member's sense of responsibility for learning, we suggest using a Jigsaw structure:

1. Form groups of three. Together, review the first lesson (Figure 2.3), the teacher's planning forms for this lesson (Figure 2.4), and the completed column for this lesson on the Jigsaw Organizer (Figure 2.2). You and your partners will be completing the remaining columns on the Jigsaw Organizer.

2. Assign one lesson to each member of the group. Each member reads his or her lesson in detail and uses the Jigsaw Organizer (Figure 2.2) to make notes about each phase of the lesson.

3. All members present the lesson they read to the group, making sure to explain what happened in each phase of the lesson.

4. While listening to each presentation, members should take notes about each lesson on the Jigsaw Organizer (Figure 2.2).

Teacher Talk: A Word About Purpose

When you look at the teachers' planning forms for the sample lessons, you'll notice that each used a special framework for defining the purpose of his or her lesson that looks like this:

Knowledge	**Habits of Mind***
What key information and facts do students need to know?	What habits of mind do you want to foster?
Understanding	**Skills**
What big ideas, generalizations, or principles do students need to understand?	What skills do students need to develop?

We call this framework a *learning window* (Silver & Perini, 2010), and we have found that using it to clarify purpose leads to richer, more integrated, and better-designed lessons.

*For a complete list of the 16 habits of mind, see Appendix B (p. 69).

Figure 2.2 **Activity: Jigsaw Organizer**

Classroom Phase	Sample Lesson 1	Sample Lesson 2	Sample Lesson 3	Sample Lesson 4
Description How did the teacher introduce the lesson and establish its purpose? What sources of information and criteria were used?	She starts with a discussion about why people exaggerate and connects the discussion to the tall tales. Sources: Pecos Bill and Paul Bunyan Criteria: character, setting, exaggerations			
Comparison What kind of organizer was used?	A Y Organizer (also: a Description Organizer in the description phase)			
Conclusion What questions or activities were used to help students draw conclusions?	Are the two tales more similar or more different? Why are tall tale heroes exaggerated?			
Application What task was used to help students synthesize their learning?	Students write an "I think" essay that argues for or against: *The heroes in tall tales are like today's superheroes.*			

Figure 2.3   **Sample Lesson 1. Elementary English/Language Arts:
What Can Tall Tales Tell Us?**

Lesson Overview

The Four Phases of Compare & Contrast	Lesson: What Can Tall Tales Tell Us?
1. Description: Students observe and describe each item separately. *Teacher Planning:* • What is the purpose for this comparison? • What sources of information will my students use? • How will I help students identify the criteria they need to focus their description? • How will I introduce the lesson?	**1.** As part of a unit on American tall tales, Gabby Sanzo is reading the tales of Paul Bunyan and Pecos Bill with her 2nd graders. Gabby begins by working with students to define *exaggeration* and asks students to share some experiences in which they or someone they know exaggerated. Then Gabby asks, "Why do people exaggerate?" After collecting students' ideas, Gabby explains that they are going to be reading a kind of story called a tall tale that uses exaggeration to make the characters seem bigger or more powerful than ordinary people. Gabby first reads the two tall tales aloud as students follow along. Then, as students read on their own, she helps them collect information from each tall tale using three questions: 1. What is the character like? (values/personality) 2. What is the setting like? 3. How is the character exaggerated?
2. Comparison: Students use a visual organizer to identify similarities and differences between items. *Teacher Planning:* • What sort of visual organizer will students use to record their comparisons?	**2.** Next, Gabby has students use the information they collected to identify the similarities and differences between the two tall tales. Gabby shows her students how to record this information on a Y Organizer. (See Step 2 on the following page.)

3. Conclusion: Students discuss the relationship between items.
 	
Teacher Planning:
 	
• Design discussion questions that will help students draw conclusions. For example,
 	
  1) Are the items more alike or different?
 	
  2) What is the most important difference? What are potential causes/effects of this difference?
 	
  3) What conclusions can you draw?
	3. For the discussion, Gabby poses this question: "Are the two tales more similar or more different?" After a few minutes of discussion, Gabby asks students to speculate as to why the heroes of tall tales might be exaggerated by their authors.

4. Application: Students apply what they have learned through the comparison. *Teacher Planning:* • Create a task that will help students synthesize their learning.	**4.** To help her students synthesize what they have learned, Gabby asks them to think about superheroes. Together, Gabby and her students come up with some ideas about what superheroes do and their powers/abilities. Gabby then writes, "The heroes in tall tales are like today's superheroes" on the board. She helps her students generate some ideas about how the statement might be interpreted as true or false before asking them to write a one-paragraph "I think" essay. Student essays must begin with either "I think the heroes in tall tales are like today's superheroes" or "I think the heroes in tall tales are not like today's superheroes."

Figure 2.4   **Teacher's Planning Form for "What Can Tall Tales Tell Us?"**

Step 1: Description

Identify the Lesson's . . .

Purpose:

Knowledge	Habits of Mind
Students will know • The critical attributes of tall tales. • What exaggeration means.	Students will develop the habits of • Applying past knowledge to new situations. • Thinking and communicating with clarity and precision.
Understanding	**Skills**
Students will understand • That tall tales use exaggeration to make their characters seem larger than life. • That the heroes people create can tell us about the times.	Students will be able to • Use criteria to describe and compare stories and characters. • Write a basic thesis ("I think") essay.

Sources:

• A reading of Paul Bunyan
• A reading of Pecos Bill

How Will You Introduce the Lesson?

We will begin with a discussion about exaggeration. I'll ask students if they have heard of it, help them define it using examples, and ask them to generate their own examples. Then I'll connect our discussion to tall tales.

Criteria:

Students will use three questions to guide their comparisons:

• What is the character like?
• What is the setting like?
• How is the character exaggerated?

Step 2: Comparison

Develop a visual organizer for students to record their description and comparison.

Description Organizer			**Comparison Organizer**
Paul Bunyan	**Criteria**	**Pecos Bill**	

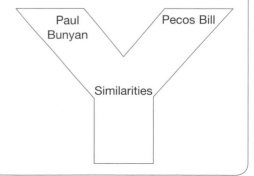

Paul Bunyan	Criteria	Pecos Bill
	Character's Values/ Personality	
	Setting	
	Exaggeration of Character	

Figure 2.4 (*continued*)

Step 3: Conclusion

Design discussion questions to help students draw conclusions.

Students will consider two questions:

1. Are the two stories more alike or more different?

2. Why do you think the heroes of tall tales were exaggerated by their authors?

Students will describe and discuss the stories, what life was like for the people in each story, and some reasons why they think the heroes were exaggerated. I'll help them connect the details of the stories to the exaggerations. (Hard work and a hard life make strength valuable.)

Step 4: Application

Create a task that will help students synthesize their learning.

Students will think about superheroes they see on television or in movies or read about in comic books and start to generate ideas about what these characters typically do and the powers and abilities they possess.

After students have thought about modern superheroes, I will have them respond to this statement: "The heroes in tall tales are like today's superheroes."

Finally, students will write a short "I think" essay in which they explain why they agree or disagree with the statement.

Figure 2.5 **Sample Lesson 2. Middle School Math:
It's in Your Interest to Know About Interest**

Lesson Overview

The Four Phases of Compare & Contrast	Lesson: It's in Your Interest to Know About Interest
1. Description: Students observe and describe each item separately. *Teacher Planning:* • What is the purpose for this comparison? • What sources of information will my students use? • How will I help students identify the criteria they need to focus their description? • How will I introduce the lesson?	**1.** As part of her unit on money and math, Maggie Bishop is teaching a lesson called "It's in Your Interest to Know About Interest." She presents students with two readings: one describes simple interest and the other describes compound interest. Both readings include the mathematical procedures for calculating each type of interest. Students read the two pieces on their own, and then work with a partner to fill out a Description Organizer for "simple interest" and "compound interest" using these criteria: *definition, purpose, how it's computed,* and *result.*
2. Comparison: Students use a visual organizer to identify similarities and differences between items. *Teacher Planning:* • What sort of visual organizer will students use to record their comparisons?	**2.** Once students have finished describing simple and compound interest, Maggie asks them to return to the readings. Students use a Top Hat Organizer to identify the important similarities and differences between the two types of interest. (See Step 2 on the following page.)
3. Conclusion: Students discuss the relationship between items. *Teacher Planning:* • Design discussion questions that will help students draw conclusions. For example: 1) Are the items more alike or different? 2) What is the most important difference? What are potential causes/effects of this difference? 3) What conclusions can you draw?	**3.** After students compare and contrast both types of interest, Maggie presents them with two graphs. Students have to determine which graph represents which type of interest and explain how they arrived at their answers. Students then discuss the respective advantages and disadvantages of simple and compound interest, and when each might be used.
4. Application: Students apply what they have learned through the comparison. *Teacher Planning:* • Create a task that will help students synthesize their learning.	**4.** For a synthesis task, Maggie presents her students with two scenarios. The first scenario asks students to invest a $500 graduation gift. The second scenario has students repay a five-year car loan. Students need to apply what they have learned about simple and compound interest to make the most financially sound decision.

Figure 2.6 Teacher's Planning Form for "It's in Your Interest to Know About Interest"

Step 1: Description

Identify the Lesson's . . .

Purpose:

Knowledge	Habits of Mind
Students will know • How to calculate simple and compound interest.	Students will develop the habits of • Striving for accuracy. • Applying past knowledge to new situations.
Understanding	**Skills**
Students will understand • When it is best to use simple interest and compound interest.	Students will be able to • Analyze real-world scenarios and data and use their analyses to make informed decisions.

Sources:
• Two short readings on simple interest and compound interest

How Will You Introduce the Lesson?

I'll start by presenting the title of the lesson: "It's in Your Interest to Know About Interest." Then I'll survey students' ideas about interest. What is it? Why is it important to understand it? When and where is it used?

Criteria:

Students will use four key questions as the criteria for their Description Organizers:
• What is it?
• What is its purpose?
• How is it computed?
• What does the result look like?

Step 2: Comparison

Develop a visual organizer for students to record their description and comparison.

Description Organizer

Simple Interest	Criteria	Compound Interest
	Definition	
	Purpose	
	How It's Computed	
	Result	

Comparison Organizer

Simple Interest	Compound Interest

Similarities

Figure 2.6 (*continued*)

Step 3: Conclusion

Design discussion questions to help students draw conclusions.

1. Look at the two graphs. Which one represents simple interest, and which one represents compound interest? How can you tell?

2. What are the advantages of compound interest over simple interest? Are there any disadvantages?

3. When might you use simple interest? When might you use compound interest?

Step 4: Application

Create a task that will help students synthesize their learning.

Students will be asked to put themselves into two different scenarios: the first scenario gives them $500 that they need to invest for four years until they graduate; the second scenario gives them an $8,000 loan for a used car that they need to pay back over five years.

Students have to analyze each scenario and determine which type of interest—simple or compound—would make the most sense for them financially.

Figure 2.7   Sample Lesson 3. High School Physical Education/Science: Aerobic vs. Anaerobic: What Is Exercise?

Lesson Overview

The Four Phases of Compare & Contrast	Lesson: Aerobic vs. Anaerobic: What Is Exercise?
1. Description: Students observe and describe each item separately. *Teacher Planning:* • What is the purpose for this comparison? • What sources of information will my students use? • How will I help students identify the criteria they need to focus their description? • How will I introduce the lesson?	1. Erika Gardino teaches physical education and wants her students to learn the scientific principles of aerobic and anaerobic exercise. She presents her class with a scenario: two students—Carly, a cross-country runner, and James, a weight lifter—are arguing about what it means to exercise and claiming that what the other does is just an "activity." After a few minutes of discussion, Erika provides students with two different ways of learning about exercise. First, she has students experience two kinds of activities for 90 seconds each: jogging in place (aerobic) and repeatedly squeezing a ball with one hand (anaerobic). Second, Erika provides a reading that explains how the body responds to aerobic and anaerobic exercise. Students use a Description Organizer to compare both types of exercise according to these criteria: *definition, examples, body's response,* and *health benefits.*
2. Comparison: Students use a visual organizer to identify similarities and differences between items. *Teacher Planning:* • What sort of visual organizer will students use to record their comparisons?	2. Using the same criteria, Erika has students compare and contrast aerobic and anaerobic exercise using a T-Shirt Organizer. Students use what they learned from the reading and draw on their own experiences to help them make their comparisons. (See Step 2 on the following page.)
3. Conclusion: Students discuss the relationship between items. *Teacher Planning:* • Design discussion questions that will help students draw conclusions. For example: 　1) Are the items more alike or different? 　2) What is the most important difference? What are potential causes/effects of this difference? 　3) What conclusions can you draw?	3. Afterward, Erika returns to the initial argument. Students discuss what exercise is, why both aerobic and anaerobic exercise are needed, why both are beneficial for good conditioning, and some situations in which one type of exercise might be more important.
4. Application: Students apply what they have learned through the comparison. *Teacher Planning:* • Create a task that will help students synthesize their learning.	4. For a synthesis task, Erika has students design a five-day conditioning program that will help them with their favorite sport. Students need to incorporate aerobic exercises and anaerobic exercises into their programs and explain how the activities they include are beneficial for their sport.

Figure 2.8 **Teacher's Planning Form for "Aerobic vs. Anaerobic: What Is Exercise?"**

Step 1: Description

Identify the Lesson's . . .

Purpose:

Knowledge	Habits of Mind
Students will know	Students will develop the habits of
• What aerobic and anaerobic activities are.	• Applying past knowledge to new situations. • Gathering data through all senses.

Understanding	Skills
Students will understand	Students will be able to
• That both aerobic and anaerobic exercise are crucial to physical conditioning. • That there is complex science behind physical education.	• Develop a sound exercise and conditioning program.

Sources:

- Reading on aerobic and anaerobic exercise
- Stopwatch (for timing)
- Small stress balls, one for each student

Criteria:

- Definition
- Examples
- Body's response
- Health benefits

How Will You Introduce the Lesson?

I'll present a scenario about two arguing athletes—a cross-country runner and a weight lifter. Each claims that what the other does is just an activity and not exercise. I'll ask students what they think about the argument. I'll also have them experience both aerobic activity (jogging in place) and anaerobic activity (squeezing a ball repeatedly) to help them formulate an initial response.

Step 2: Comparison

Develop a visual organizer for students to record their description and comparison.

Description Organizer

Aerobic Exercise	Criteria	Anaerobic Exercise
	Definition	
	Examples	
	Body's Response	
	Health Benefits	

Comparison Organizer

Figure 2.8 (*continued*)

Step 3: Conclusion

Design discussion questions to help students draw conclusions.

1. What is aerobic exercise? What is anaerobic exercise?

2. Why are both aerobic and anaerobic exercise needed?

3. How are both types of exercise beneficial for good conditioning?

4. Are there certain sports or activities in which one type of exercise is more important than the other?

Step 4: Application

Create a task that will help students synthesize their learning.

Students will review what they have learned about aerobic and anaerobic exercise. They will select a sport that interests them and use what they have learned to design a five-day conditioning program. Students need to incorporate both aerobic and anaerobic exercises into their programs and explain why they selected each exercise and how each is beneficial to conditioning for their chosen sport.

Figure 2.9 **Sample Lesson 4. High School English/U.S. History: Poetry of the Civil Rights Movement**

Lesson Overview

The Four Phases of Compare & Contrast	**Lesson:** Poetry of the Civil Rights Movement
1. Description: Students observe and describe each item separately. *Teacher Planning:* • What is the purpose for this comparison? • What sources of information will my students use? • How will I help students identify the criteria they need to focus their description? • How will I introduce the lesson?	**1.** Charles Lester's 9th grade U.S. history class is starting a unit on the Civil Rights Movement. He wants his students to understand the evolution of the feelings and motivations behind the movement. He hands out three poems: "We Wear the Mask" by Paul Laurence Dunbar (1895); "If We Must Die" by Claude McKay (1919); and "Theme for English B" by Langston Hughes (1951). In their learning groups, students read the poems aloud and discuss the mood of each poem, themes they find, and the emotions portrayed. Students are also encouraged to discuss personal experiences or situations in which they felt similar emotions. After discussion, Charles asks students to speculate on the chronological order of the poems.
2. Comparison: Students use a visual organizer to identify similarities and differences between items. *Teacher Planning:* • What sort of visual organizer will students use to record their comparisons?	**2.** Next, Charles has his students use a Matrix Organizer to identify similarities and differences between the poems. (See Step 2 on the following page.)
3. Conclusion: Students discuss the relationship between items. *Teacher Planning:* • Design discussion questions that will help students draw conclusions. For example: 1) Are the items more alike or different? 2) What is the most important difference? What are potential causes/effects of this difference? 3) What conclusions can you draw?	**3.** Charles reveals the correct chronological order of the poems. Students check their predictions against the correct order. Then Charles uses the following discussion questions to help students explore how the themes and moods evolved over time through three different poets: • Which poem do you like most, and why? What does the poem tell you about the Civil Rights Movement? • How do the poets capture the mood of the time in their poetry? • How did the themes and moods of the Civil Rights Movement evolve over time?
4. Application: Students apply what they have learned through the comparison. *Teacher Planning:* • Create a task that will help students synthesize their learning.	**4.** To help his students synthesize what they have learned, Charles asks them to pick their favorite of the three poems and to mimic its structure and style to tell how they once reacted to an unjust or unfair situation.

Figure 2.10   **Teacher's Planning Form for "Poetry of the Civil Rights Movement"**

Step 1: Description

Identify the Lesson's . . .

Purpose:

Knowledge	Habits of Mind
Students will know	Students will develop the habits of
• Basic elements of a poem: theme, mood, feelings. • Authors and chronology of the three poems.	• Listening with understanding and empathy. • Creating, imagining, and innovating.
Understanding	**Skills**
Students will understand	Students will be able to
• That poetry is a powerful form for expressing ideas about social injustice.	• Use poetry to analyze historical events. • Write a personal poem.

Sources:

Three poems by three African American poets:

• "We Wear the Mask" by Paul Laurence Dunbar

• "If We Must Die" by Claude McKay

• "Theme for English B" by Langston Hughes

Criteria:

• Mood

• Themes

• Emotions portrayed

How Will You Introduce the Lesson?

My plan is to let students work in learning groups and to let the power and emotion of the three short poems speak for themselves. I'll encourage students to focus on feelings—those in the poems and their own feelings, too. I'll also challenge them to see if they can figure out the chronological order of the poems.

Step 2: Comparison

Develop a visual organizer for students to record their description and comparison.

Students will use the following organizer to record differences and similarities.

	"We Wear the Mask"	"If We Must Die"	"Theme for English B"	Similarities
Mood				
Themes				
Emotions				

Figure 2.10 (*continued*)

Step 3: Conclusion

Design discussion questions to help students draw conclusions.

1. Which poem do you like most, and why? What does the poem tell you about the Civil Rights Movement?

2. How do the poets capture the mood of the time in their poetry?

3. How did the themes and moods of the Civil Rights Movement evolve over time?

Students will be asked to compare their rankings with the actual chronological order of the poems and discuss, in small groups, what the actual order says about the Civil Rights Movement and how it evolved.

Step 4: Application

Create a task that will help students synthesize their learning.

Students will be asked to write a poem that reflects their own personal experience in dealing with injustice. Students will use the structure and style of their favorite of the three poems as their model.

Compare & Contrast Planning Forms

Now you are going to plan your own lesson using the Compare & Contrast strategy. You will be using the content you brought when you started this section to create the lesson. As you move through the planning forms that follow on pages 42–44, keep the principles and phases of Compare & Contrast in mind because they will help to focus and enrich your lesson. To further help you align your content to your standards, we have added a "Standards to Address" field to the first phase. (*Remember to photocopy these planning forms so that you can use them to plan future lessons.*)

Planning Phase 1: Description

Identify the lesson's . . .

Standards to Address:

Purpose:

Knowledge	Habits of Mind
Understanding	**Skills**

Sources:

Criteria:

How Will You Introduce the Lesson?

Planning Phase 2: Comparison

Develop a visual organizer for students to record their description and comparison.

Description Organizer

Comparison Organizer

Examples for comparison:

Planning Phase 3: Conclusion

Design discussion questions to help students draw conclusions.

1.

2.

3.

4.

Planning Phase 4: Application

Create a task that will help students synthesize their learning.

Classroom Tips

In this section, you will find tips for getting the most out of your Compare & Contrast lesson in your classroom.

Introducing Compare & Contrast to Your Students

When you first introduce the strategy, students of all ages, but especially younger students, will need some teacher modeling to see how you describe items using criteria and compare items by identifying similarities and differences. Use think-alouds (thinking out loud while you go through the process) to help students hear the kinds of questions they should be asking themselves as they describe and compare items.

Also, students often need to try their hands at the Compare & Contrast strategy using content that's a little closer to home than, say, two poems by Robert Frost. Lead students through the four phases using concrete objects first. Comparing and contrasting items as simple as different kinds of shoes or food is a good way to introduce comparative thinking. (Don't forget criteria!) Use the included poster to teach students the phases in the strategy.

Phase One: Description

• Use a hook to capture student interest and help students apply their past knowledge to learning to come: "What do we mean when we say an artist has a unique style? What influences an artist's style?"

• Bridge the discussion generated by the hook to the purpose for the lesson: "You have some wonderful ideas about how artists develop their own styles. Today, we're going to use the Compare & Contrast strategy to learn how two famous 20th century artists—Picasso and Matisse—developed their own revolutionary styles of art."

• Clearly state the criteria for describing items. Remind students that they are describing the items separately, not comparing them yet. Use a simple description organizer to help students collect relevant information (see Figure 2.11).

• As students become more comfortable with the strategy, work with them to preview content and generate their own criteria. Remind students to strive for accuracy as they track down and record information.

Figure 2.11 **A Simple Description Organizer**

Picasso	Criteria	Matisse
	Influences Theory of Art Stylistic Innovations	

Phase Two: Comparison

• Make sure each student has his or her own visual organizer, and remind students to line up related differences side by side (see Figure 2.12).

• In early applications, consider having students work together in small groups so that they can think interdependently and pool the results of their work from the description phase.

• Keep students focused on significant, rather than trivial, details. Use the criteria from the description phase to help clarify the difference between the significant and the trivial. Once again, accuracy counts.

Phase Three: Conclusion

The point of the conclusion phase is to extend students' thoughts through discussion. Once you pose the discussion questions you designed for this phase, use the Q-SPACE techniques below to deepen the discussion and foster critical habits of mind, including questioning, listening with understanding, thinking flexibly, and metacognition.

• **Q**uestion: Pose your question and make sure all students understand what you're asking.

• **S**ilence: Wait time is important. Give students five seconds of silence to find or extend their ideas.

• **P**robe: Say things like "Tell me more" and "How did you come up with that idea?" to help students expose and articulate their thinking. Ask students to present evidence to support their responses.

• **A**ccept: Accept every answer, but keep the discussion going by not affirming or correcting students' thoughts. Affirmation and correction signal the end of the question-and-answer cycle to many students.

• **C**larify: Ask students to restate their own—and other students'—ideas.

• **E**laborate: Work with students to go further and deeper with their ideas. Try using "What if?" questions or ask students to respond to counterarguments. Encourage students to draw conclusions and refine them through further discussion.

Figure 2.12   **Comparison Organizer (Top Hat)**

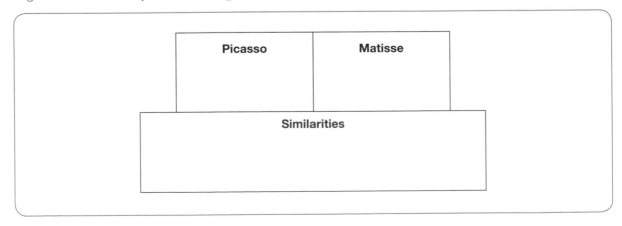

Phase Four: Application

The most obvious application is to have students use what they have learned to write a comparative essay. Comparative essays are among the most common essay forms and are featured on many state and national tests. Work with students to help them convert their comparisons into clear comparative essays. Teach them how to use transitional words and phrases associated with comparing and contrasting:

But	Either . . . or	Similar to
On the other hand	Neither . . . nor	Different from
However	Although	More than
Nonetheless	In contrast to	Less than
Not only . . . but also	Compared to	Have in common
Yet	While	Alike

Students—especially younger students—developing their first few comparison essays will benefit from a simple writing framework like the one shown below, which provides a clear structure for communicating their ideas with clarity and precision.

Simple Comparative Writing Framework

I am comparing and contrasting _____ and _____.

Although _____ and _____ are different, they are

alike in some ways. For example, _____ and _____

are both _____. There are also some interesting differences between

_____ and _____.

For example, _____.

[Concluding sentence:] _____.

Of course, there are many other kinds of application tasks you can use to help students synthesize and demonstrate their learning. Throughout this guide, you'll find teachers who designed tasks asking students to

• Create a "Flip Strip" to show how frogs and toads differ (p. 10).

• Write an "I think" essay arguing for or against this statement: *The heroes in tall tales are like today's superheroes* (p. 32).

• Examine real-world scenarios and use what they have learned about simple and compound interest to make financially sound decisions (p. 35).

• Design a personal conditioning program that includes both aerobic and anaerobic activity (p. 38).

• Write a poem in the style of a famous poet expressing a personal reaction to an unjust situation (p. 41).

THOUGHTWORK

Before the Next Section

Between this section and the next, you should teach your Compare & Contrast lesson in your own classroom. Take some time to review and refine the lesson that you created while working through this section. As you prepare the lesson, consider the questions below.

Activity: Rooting Out Problems

1. What types of problems might you encounter while teaching this lesson?

2. What patterns do you see as you think about these potential problems?

3. Select one type of problem. What are the facts you know about this problem?

4. What are some of the possible causes for this type of problem?

5. What is the best solution to this problem?

THOUGHTWORK

When it comes to improving the quality of instruction, there are few resources more valuable than a critical friend who listens to your thinking, observes your work, and offers constructive feedback to help you get better results in the classroom. That's why we strongly recommend that you select a critical friend and schedule time to observe each other in the classroom. The two of you should take turns: you present your lesson to your class while your partner takes notes. Then switch roles. Use the questions below to structure your observation notes. When you start Section 3, be prepared to share what you have learned as a result of implementing and observing a Compare & Contrast lesson.

Activity: Observation Notes

Description

1. How was the lesson introduced?

2. How did the students approach the task of describing each item separately?

3. How did the students make use of the criteria?

Comparison

1. What kind of visual organizer did the students use?

2. What patterns did you notice in students' work as they identified similarities and differences?

Conclusion

1. What question was used to open up the discussion? To focus and guide the discussion?

2. How would you describe student participation in and contributions to the discussion?

Application

1. What task was used to help students apply what they learned from the comparison?

2. What differences did you notice among students' responses to the application task?

Evaluating the Lesson

Our goal in this section is to deepen our understanding of the Compare & Contrast strategy by working in teams to reflect on the strategy and refine our use of it in the classroom.

In this section you will

- Share your experiences implementing and observing Compare & Contrast in the classroom.

- Reflect more deeply on your own lesson by exploring specific questions related to each of the four Compare & Contrast phases.

Sharing Your Experience

Now that you have presented a lesson using the Compare & Contrast strategy and observed one of your peers doing the same, it's time to share what you have learned with your learning club. We recommend following the steps below:

Step 1: Using the observation questions provided in Section 2's ThoughtWork as a guide, present your observations of *your partner's* lesson to the group.

Step 2: When you are finished, your partner will comment on the challenges and successes he or she experienced while presenting his or her lesson.

Step 3: Next, switch roles so that your partner can present his or her observations of *your* lesson.

Step 4: Now it's your turn to share the challenges and successes you experienced with your own lesson.

Consider the following questions when you share your thoughts on your own lesson.

Activity: Reflecting on Your Compare & Contrast Lesson

1. **What goal did you set out to achieve?**

2. **What steps did you take? What was hard for you?**

3. **What came naturally?**

4. **What worked about the lesson, and what just wouldn't work?**

After the presentations to the group, meet again with your partner to discuss the notes you both made. What stood out in your partner's lesson? What questions did the lesson raise for you? How might you improve upon your partner's lesson?

Now consider the feedback your partner gave you. Use the space below to expand on your partner's ideas for how to improve your lesson. Include what you thought you did well, how your students responded to the lesson, and what you might do differently next time.

Activity: Improving Your Next Compare & Contrast Lesson

How might you improve your lesson?

For the ThoughtWork activity on the next page, you will design a second Compare & Contrast lesson for your classroom. You may choose to begin planning now as part of a learning club meeting, or you may prefer to plan on your own or with your critical friend outside the meeting.

THOUGHTWORK

Before the Next Section

Before the final section, complete the following tasks:

• Plan another lesson using the Compare & Contrast strategy. Use the planning forms provided on pages 42–44 to guide you. We have also provided some sample comparison topics in various content areas to inspire you (see Figure 2.1, pp. 26–27).

• Present the lesson to your students.

• Collect three samples of student work from your lesson and bring them to the next meeting. The student work you collect should reflect what you believe to be three distinct levels of achievement: high, middle, and low (or expert, proficient, and apprentice).

• Bring enough copies of your student work to distribute to the members of your learning club.

Learning from Student Work

Our goal in this section is to examine student work at various levels of proficiency and use it to help us refine our work in designing and delivering Compare & Contrast lessons.

In this section you will

- See how a teacher selected and analyzed her three samples of student work.

- Share and discuss the student work you collected from the last section.

- Develop a rubric for assessing student work based on your discussion and samples.

- Plan your next steps in building students' comparative analysis skills.

Examining Samples

In this final section, you are going to use student work to assess the effectiveness of your instruction, your students' comparative analysis skills, and your students' grasp of the content. Let's start with a model to guide your examination of the student work you collected for this section. Here are three 4th graders' essays comparing bats and birds.

Figure 4.1 **Three Levels of Student Work: How Are Bats and Birds Similar and Different?**

Expert

While there are actually many differences between bats and birds, at first glance, bats and birds appear to be very similar creatures. The most obvious reason for this is that both birds and bats have wings and can fly. Birds and bats are also often similar in size. Another reason why birds and bats look similar is that they are both vertebrates, which means that they both have backbones. If you take a closer look, however, you will find that there are actually many important differences between bats and birds. Although birds and bats look similar from far away, birds are covered with feathers while bats are covered with fur. Additionally, bats are mammals but birds are not. Like other mammals, bats have live babies. In contrast, birds lay eggs instead. Birds and bats also have different types of homes. For example, bats live in caves, whereas birds live in nests. Finally, while birds are active during the day, bats are nocturnal animals, which means that they come out at night. So although birds and bats may look similar at first, they are really not that much alike after all.

Proficient

I used to think bats and birds were the same but now I know they are different. Birds and bats are very similar. For example both can fly. Bats and birds also have some interesting differences between them. One example is bats fly around in the dark at night and live in caves. Birds are afraid of the dark so they come out at daytime and they don't go into caves. That is why birds live in nests. Another interesting difference is that birds lay eggs and bats don't. Another interesting similarity is that both bats and birds eat some of the same things, but bats eat blood and birds don't. Another interesting difference between bats and birds is that birds are birds and bats aren't. Finally, birds sleep with their heads up but bats hang upside down. How would you like to eat blood and sleep during the day upside down?

Apprentice

Birds and bats are both animals and they can fly. Birds and bats are the same size, so that is one reason they are the same. But bats are black and birds are not black. Also birds probably don't have teeth. These are reasons bats and birds are different. For example, birds have beaks and bats don't. Birds and bats like to eat the same food. But bats also eat blood. Bats like being awake at night and birds sleep during the night like I do. That is a difference. Another difference is because birds lay eggs and bats live in caves. Bats would probably win if they got in a fight with a bird.

Take a moment to examine your thinking about the student work samples you have just reviewed. What do you notice about the expert sample that is missing from the other two? Which criteria might you use to compare these levels, and how might you describe each sample based on those criteria? Record your thoughts below.

Activity: Reflecting on Sample Student Work

Possible criteria:

The teacher who gave the essay task on bats and birds created the rubric in Figure 4.2 to guide her assessment of student work. You may want to use this rubric as a model when you develop your own rubric later in this section.

Figure 4.2   Teacher's Rubric for Bats and Birds Essay

	High Performance	Average Performance	Low or Struggling Performance
Content	<ul><li>Includes critical attributes of both bats and birds.</li><li>Clearly identifies the critical similarities and differences between bats and birds.</li><li>Includes all relevant information from the organizer.</li></ul>	<ul><li>Recognizes most of the important attributes of both bats and birds.</li><li>Identifies some similarities between bats and birds.</li><li>Includes most of the information from the organizer.</li></ul>	<ul><li>Limited recognition of key attributes of bats and birds.</li><li>Similarities and differences between bats and birds are limited or focused on irrelevant information.</li><li>Minimal use of information taken from the organizer.</li></ul>
Process	<ul><li>Items are compared and contrasted clearly.</li><li>The writing uses specific examples to show the comparison.</li></ul>	<ul><li>The writing compares and contrasts some items clearly, but details are often general.</li></ul>	<ul><li>The writing attempts a comparison, but details are often incomplete, missing altogether, or focused mostly on either the similarities or the differences.</li></ul>
Product	<ul><li>Sophisticated use of transitions.</li><li>Strong introduction and conclusion.</li><li>Uses strong and varied sentence structure.</li><li>Follows standard conventions of English for spelling, grammar, etc.</li></ul>	<ul><li>Some use of transitions.</li><li>Solid introduction and conclusion.</li><li>Some sentence variety.</li><li>Few grammatical or spelling mistakes; good use of standard conventions.</li></ul>	<ul><li>Limited or total lack of transitions.</li><li>Weak introduction and/or conclusion.</li><li>Sentences may be simple or incomplete.</li><li>Weak command of standard English conventions for spelling, grammar, etc.</li></ul>

Let's now turn to your thought process in selecting your own student work samples. Take a few minutes to reexamine your samples, keeping in mind the following questions:

- How did you select work from each level?

- Which criteria did you use to choose this work?

Record your thoughts in the space provided below.

Activity: How You Selected Student Work Samples

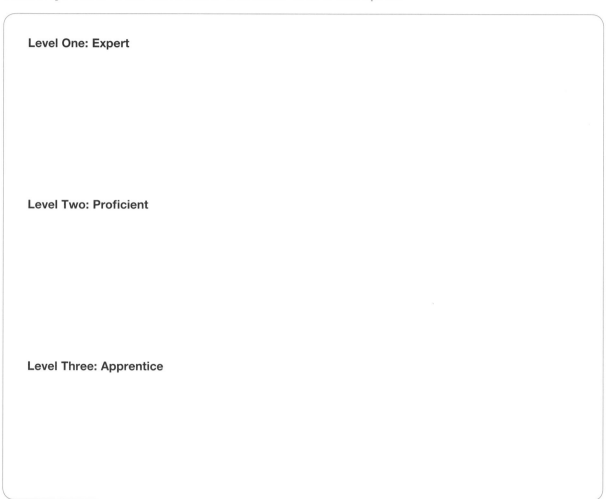

Level One: Expert

Level Two: Proficient

Level Three: Apprentice

Next, meet with your partner to share the student work you collected. Work together to analyze the content, process, and product of the student work. Keep in mind that examining this student work is less about whether commas and semicolons are in the right place and more about how well your students have put their understanding of the content and the comparative process to work.

Note that we have provided two different formats for this collaborative analysis of student work. Option 1 uses various questions to guide the analysis. Option 2 uses a rubric format. Decide which format works better for you and your partner and use it to conduct your analysis.

Activity: Analyzing Student Work, Option 1—Questions

Content

1. What does the student work in comparison suggest about students' grasp of the key ideas and details?

2. Which parts of the content are firmly in their grasp?

3. Which ideas and details are slipping through the cracks?

Process

1. What does this work suggest about how your students describe, compare, and synthesize?

2. How do they use criteria? Do they note and make use of big ideas and important details?

Product

1. What similarities and differences do you notice in the quality of student work?

2. How well are students communicating their ideas?

3. What signs are there that students are reaching toward excellence? What patterns of strength and weakness do you find compelling?

Activity: Analyzing Student Work, Option 2—Rubric

	High Performance	Average Performance	Low or Struggling Performance
Content			
Process			
Product			

Now, summarize what you have learned from your analysis and plan your next steps.

Activity: Thinking About the Next Steps

Content

What have you learned about your students' grasp of ideas and details in the content area?

Process

What have you learned about your students' ability to describe, compare, and synthesize learning?

Product

What have you learned about your students' ability to communicate? What motivates them to reach toward excellence?

Interventions

How will you use these insights? What kinds of instructional interventions do you need to make?*

*For a collection of ready-to-use instructional techniques for helping students meet your benchmarks, see *Tools for Promoting Active, In-Depth Learning* (Silver, Strong, & Perini, 2001).

Where Am I Now?

Before completing this guide, take a few minutes to think about your own grasp of the Compare & Contrast strategy. Looking at the strategy implementation milestones below, where do you think you are now? What do you need to do to move to the next level?

Strategy Implementation Milestones

✓   I know what Compare & Contrast is and can describe what it looks like in the classroom.

✓   I understand Compare & Contrast and can explain how it works.

✓   I have planned several Compare & Contrast lessons, used them in my classroom, and reflected with my colleagues on their effects on my students.

✓   My students have a solid understanding of Compare & Contrast, and I can see them transferring the thinking skills involved in the strategy to other situations.

✓   I am ready to teach other people how to use Compare & Contrast.

Appendix A: The Power of Similarities and Differences

Compare & Contrast is one strategy in a family of four that Robert Marzano and his team refer to as "Identifying Similarities and Differences" (Marzano, 2007; Marzano et al., 2001). Their research has shown that strategies that engage students in comparative thinking consistently yield high levels of student achievement. Here, we provide a brief overview of the three additional comparative strategies. Each of these strategies is covered in depth in *The Strategic Teacher: Selecting the Right Research-Based Strategy for Every Lesson* (Silver, Strong, & Perini, 2007).

Inductive Learning

Inductive Learning requires students to examine a set of examples or a bank of data and develop a classification system. Figure A.1 is an example from a 6th grade mathematics class.

Figure A.1 **Student's Classification System for a Set of Numbers**

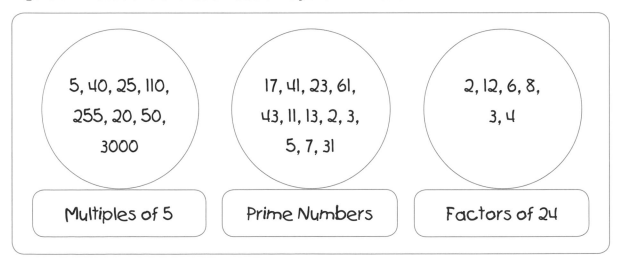

Encourage students to group items in ways that are meaningful to them. Make sure you emphasize the importance of giving each group a descriptive label. Collect and record students' ideas on the board. Students can use their groups to make predictions about the learning to come: as they encounter evidence that confirms or refutes their predictions, they record it. Lessons incorporating Inductive Learning typically culminate with a task that asks students to apply their classification system in a meaningful way.

Decision Making

Decision Making is the most personal form of comparison, inviting students into the content to examine alternatives and use their own values to make and justify a decision. Begin by identifying a set of concepts or ideas that you would like your students to consider in greater depth. For example, U.S. history teacher Jessica Alvarez wants her freshmen to analyze the presidencies of the 19th century and decide who they think was the best president of that century.

Next, work with your students to identify three to five criteria to use to evaluate the alternatives. Here are the four criteria that Jessica developed with her students:

- Major achievements

- Major crises

- Popularity

- Effect on future presidents

Jessica's students collect specific details that they use to evaluate each alternative according to their criteria (see Figure A.2). They then assign a value to each cell in their organizer using a 1–5 scale. Students add up these numerical values to make their decisions.

Figure A.2   **Student's Partial Decision-Making Matrix**

	Major Achievements	Major Crises
Lincoln	Commander in Chief during the Civil War Signed Emancipation Proclamation 5	Attack on Fort Sumter Secession of Southern States Civil War 5
Grant	Wrote a lucid and insightful autobiography General of Union Army 3	Teapot Dome Scandal Reconstruction of Former Confederacy 2

Metaphorical Expression

Metaphors engage students in deep, critical thinking by asking them to make creative comparisons and explain connections between dissimilar ideas or items.

Metaphors and similes are sneaky; they look like pairs when they are really triplets. Take the opening of Shakespeare's Sonnet 73, for example:

> *That time of year thou mayst in me behold*
> *When yellow leaves, or none, or few, do hang*
> *Upon those boughs which shake against the cold, . . .*

When you first look at the metaphor, it looks like a pair: me (the speaker) and a tree in winter (the object). However, as Figure A.3 shows, there is an invisible element to this equation.

Figure A.3   **Sonnet 73, Metaphorical Connection**

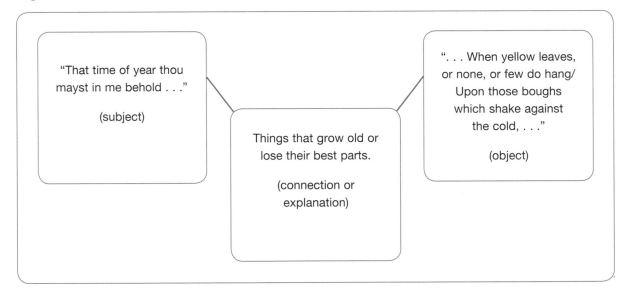

Sometimes when we are teaching students, we provide them with all three parts to help them understand a key concept (see Figure A.4).

Once students are familiar with the use of metaphors, you can begin to use them to help students review or gain new insight into your content. Begin by creating a metaphorical question based on a unit you are planning. For example, a unit on the American Revolution may contain a metaphorical question like "How was the American Revolution like an earthquake?"

Provide students with a visual organizer and ask them to jot down whatever they know about the subject and object. (You may want to provide students with a short reading or other source of information.) Then ask your students to work through as many connections as possible. Wrap up the lesson by asking students to create a product that demonstrates or explains the key concepts.

Figure A.4   **Metaphorical Connection in Earth Science**

"The earth's atmosphere . . ."

(subject)

Just like a blanket in winter, the earth's atmosphere is piled up in layers that protect us and keep us warm.

(connection)

". . . is like a blanket on your bed."

(object)

Similarities and Differences: Sample Lessons

The matrix in Figure A.5 includes a variety of lesson starters—questions and activities in four content areas—using Compare & Contrast, Inductive Learning, Decision Making, and Metaphorical Expression.

Figure A.5   **Matrix of Lesson Starters**

	Compare & Contrast	Inductive Learning	Decision Making	Metaphorical Expression
Science	How are reptiles and amphibians alike and different? Describe the similarities and differences of each by creating a Venn Diagram.	Review the list of 18 animals. First, group the animals according to biome. Next, group the animals according to class. What do you notice?	Study this list of 10 major scientific discoveries of the 20th century. Rate each discovery using a 1–10 scale (1 being most important). Write a short persuasive essay explaining why your first choice is the most important scientific discovery of the 20th century.	How is a snowflake like a fingerprint?

Figure A.5 (*continued*)

	Compare & Contrast	Inductive Learning	Decision Making	Metaphorical Expression
Mathematics	How are fractions and decimals alike and different? Use a Top Hat Organizer to collect information.	Look at the page of polygons. There are 15 shapes in total. Place the shapes into at least four groups. You must use each shape once, but you can put the same shape into different groups. Make sure you give each group a descriptive label.	Read the specifications for these three MP3 players. Analyze and rate each MP3 player according to cost of player, storage capacity, and screen size. Determine which MP3 player is the best buy for you.	Is a dartboard a good way to think about measures of central tendency? Why or why not?
Social Studies	Review the map of the 13 Original Colonies. Organize the colonies into Southern, Mid-Atlantic, and New England. Then analyze each group of colonies using the criteria on your Matrix Organizer.	Below are a list of important people, places, and concepts to help you study Ancient Egypt. Organize the 24 terms into at least five groups. Give each group a descriptive label and connect related groups.	Read over the Bill of Rights. Develop three criteria for analyzing each of the 10 amendments. Rate each amendment on a scale of 1–10, with 1 being the most important to you. If you could have only three amendments, what would they be?	Why were European allies of the Soviet Union called "satellites" during the Cold War?
English/ Language Arts	Think about the book you just read, *The House on Mango Street*. Use a Top Hat Organizer to compare and contrast the neighborhood in the story to your neighborhood.	Now that you've finished *Bridge to Terabithia,* you should be able to classify the list of characters into groups. Make sure you give each group a good label. This will help you explain the story to a friend.	Review the list of major characters in *Romeo and Juliet.* Rate each character according to his or her involvement in the final outcome of the story. Write a critical editorial for the "Verona News" explaining who you think is most at fault.	How is a literary theme like an iceberg?

Appendix B: What Are the Habits of Mind?

Habits of mind are dispositions that are skillfully and mindfully employed by characteristically intelligent, successful people when they are confronted with problems whose solutions are not immediately apparent.

The habits of mind as identified by Art Costa and Bena Kallick (2008, 2009) are

- Persisting.
- Thinking and communicating with clarity and precision.
- Managing impulsivity.
- Gathering data through all senses.
- Listening with understanding and empathy.
- Creating, imagining, and innovating.
- Thinking flexibly.
- Responding with wonderment and awe.
- Thinking about thinking (metacognition).
- Taking responsible risks.
- Striving for accuracy.
- Finding humor.
- Questioning and posing problems.
- Thinking interdependently.
- Applying past knowledge to new situations.
- Remaining open to continuous learning.

To learn more about the habits of mind and how schools across the globe are using them to improve teaching and learning, go to www.instituteforhabitsofmind.com.

References

Costa, A. L., & Kallick, B. (2008). *Learning and leading with habits of mind: 16 essential characteristics for success*. Alexandria, VA: ASCD.

Costa, A. L., & Kallick, B. (2009). *Habits of mind across the curriculum: Practical and creative strategies for teachers*. Alexandria, VA: ASCD.

Joyce, B. R., & Showers, B. (2002). *Student achievement through staff development* (3rd ed.). Alexandria, VA: ASCD.

Marzano, R. J. (2007). *The art and science of teaching: A comprehensive framework for effective instruction*. Alexandria, VA: ASCD.

Marzano, R. J., Pickering, D. J., & Pollock, J. E. (2001). *Classroom instruction that works: Research-based strategies for increasing student achievement*. Alexandria, VA: ASCD.

Schmoker, M. (2005). Here and now: Improving teaching and learning. In R. DuFour, R. Eaker, & R. DuFour (Eds.), *On common ground: The power of professional learning communities* (pp. xi–xvi). Bloomington, IN: Solution Tree.

Silver, H. F., & Perini, M. J. (2010). *Classroom curriculum design: How strategic units improve instruction and engage students in meaningful learning*. Ho-Ho-Kus, NJ: Thoughtful Education Press.

Silver, H. F., Strong, R. W., & Perini, M. J. (2001). *Tools for promoting active, in-depth learning* (2nd ed.). Ho-Ho-Kus, NJ: Thoughtful Education Press.

Silver, H. F., Strong, R. W., & Perini, M. J. (2007). *The strategic teacher: Selecting the right research-based strategy for every lesson*. Alexandria, VA: ASCD.

About the Author

Harvey F. Silver, Ed.D, is president of Silver Strong & Associates and Thoughtful Education Press. He has conducted numerous workshops for school districts and state education departments throughout the United States. He was the principal consultant for the Georgia Critical Thinking Skills Program and the Kentucky Thoughtful Education Teacher Leadership Program. He has written a number of bestsellers in education, including *The Strategic Teacher; So Each May Learn: Integrating Learning Styles and Multiple Intelligences; Teaching What Matters Most: Standards and Strategies for Raising Student Achievement;* and *Tools for Promoting Active, In-Depth Learning,* which won a Teacher's Choice Award in 2004. With the late Richard Strong, he developed The Thoughtful Classroom—a renowned professional development initiative dedicated to the goal of "Making Students as Important as Standards." Dr. Silver may be reached at Silver Strong & Associates, 227 First Street, Ho-Ho-Kus, NJ 07423; 1-800-962-4432 (T); hsilver@thoughtfulclassroom.com.